Cisco Network Essentials

Complete Guide To Computer Networking For Beginners And Intermediates

Craig Berg

Introduction

To succeed as a network engineer in the Information Technology industry, you need to know Cisco.

Before you can master complex networking concepts, you need to understand the building block of networking. In the first section of this guide, we shall discuss the basics of networking so that you can have a solid understanding of networking and are thus able to understand complex cisco networking concepts.

PS: I'd like your feedback. If you are happy with this book, please leave a review on Amazon.

Please leave a review for this book on Amazon by visiting the page below:

https://amzn.to/2VMR5qr

Cisco Networking Essentials

Your Gift

Let me help you master this and other programming stuff quickly.

Visit

https://bit.ly/codetutorials

To Find Out More

Table of Contents

Introduction _____ 2

Section 1: Networking Essentials _____ 6

#: Introduction To Networks _____ 6

Types Of Networks _____ 6

A Basic Network Model _____ 7

Section 2: OSI Model _____ 12

#: The Open Systems Interconnections Model   12

Benefits Of Dividing A Network Into Various Layers _____ 13

#: Data Encapsulation _____ 21

Section 3: TCP/IP _____ 24

#: TCP/IP _____ 24

Section 4: Ethernet Technologies And Cabling _____ 53

Section 5: Ethernet Standards _____ 66

Section 6: Data Encapsulation In TCP/IP Model_____ 72

Cisco 3 Layer Hierarchical Model _____73

Section 7: Internet Protocol Addresses ___ 78

#: IP Addresses _____ 78

Conclusion _____ 85

Section 1: Networking Essentials

#: Introduction To Networks

Wikipedia defines a computer network is "a group of two or more devices linked together so that they can communicate with each other. A device connected to a network is a "host." Modern appliances connect to a network using a network interface card or NIC.

Types Of Networks

We have several types of computer networks. The most common ones include:

Local Area Network

A local area network is a type of network where the interconnected devices are near each other, such as in the same building. The most common type of connection for LAN is an ethernet cable or a wireless connection.

Wide Area Network

A wide area network is a type of network where the connected devices are situated several kilometers from each other. The main way to connect these devices is radio waves or telephone lines.

Internet

The internet is the largest network that interconnects thousands of LANs and WANs. It is a global networking system consisting of systems owned by the government and private organizations around the world.

A Basic Network Model

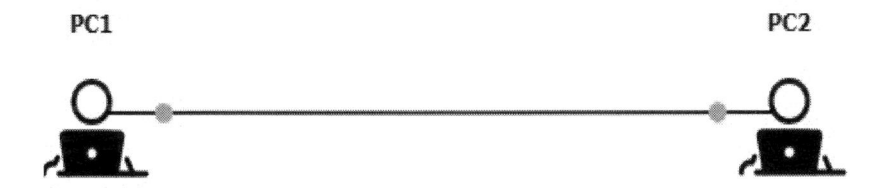

PC1   PC2

The figure above shows two interconnected computers in a simple LAN network.

On one end, the network cable connects to one PC, while on the other end, it connects to the next PC. In this simple case, these two devices have a direct connection with each other. If you need to scale the network to more than two devices, you will need a network device called a hub.

A hub is a device connected to a network to repeat all the information received from a host in the same network to all other hosts in the network.

Cisco Networking Essentials

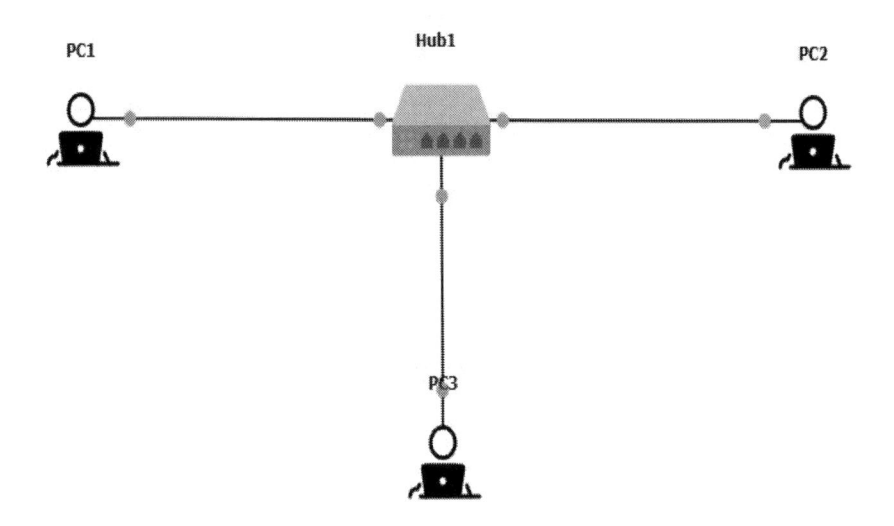

```
   PC1              Hub1                PC2
    O─────────────── ▭ ───────────────O
                     │
                     │
                    PC3
                     O
```

In the above figure, it means Hub1 will relay the information received from PC1 to PC2, PC3, and other available devices. This connection makes it possible for the transfer of data to happen between all the hosts connected to the same network. Communication between hosts in the same network falls into three main types:

1. **Unicast:** A unicast communication is a type of network communication between one host to another.

2. **Broadcast:** A broadcast is a communication made by one host to all other hosts in the network.

3. **Multicast:** A multicast is a message sent by one host to selected hosts in the network.

Various issues arise when we use a hub in a network. They include:

- A hub repeats all the information received from one host to another. If PC1 sends a unicast message to PC2, the hub will repeat this information to PC3 too, which will require PC3 to discard the message.

- A hub creates a single shared network where only one host can send data packets at a time. If two or more hosts in the networks send data packets at the same time, a collision will occur, which forces the hosts to resend the packet. We refer to this shared network medium as a single collision domain. Data packet collisions may not be a very significant problem for a network that has 3 to 4 hosts; however, for networks with more than 100 hosts, it can be a big problem that leads to the degeneration of the network.

To solve hub-related problems, we use switches instead of hubs. Unlike hubs, Switches eliminate domain collision by providing each connection a unique port, which means that each host connects to an individual port, which thus ensures that no packet collisions happen in the network.

Similarly, switches do not flood the network packets out on all ports. For a unicast packet, switches forward the packets to the destination port only.

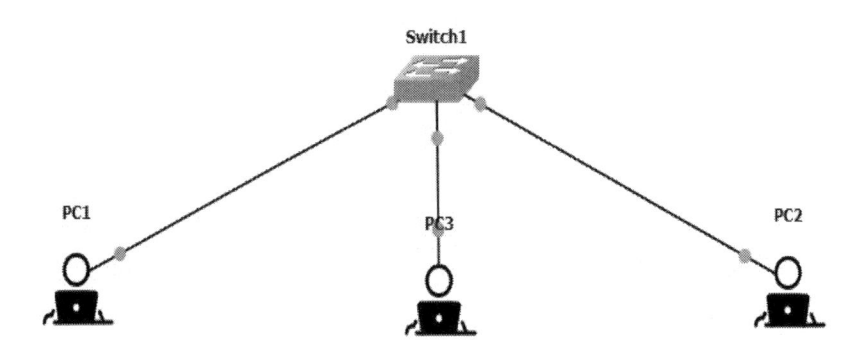

```
                    Switch1
                      ▭

   PC1               PC3                PC2
    💻               💻                 💻
```

In the Figure above —using a switch instead of hub—, if PC1 sends a unicast message to PC2, the switch will send the message to PC2 only; PC3 will not receive the packet. Switches improve and help solve problems in a network. However, the use of switches also has associated issues.

As we have discussed, hubs flood the network packets whether broadcast, unicast, or multicast. Hosts connected to a switched network are in the same broadcast domain, which means every host in the domain will receive all broadcasted packets. Although broadcast packets play a crucial role in a network, in a complex network where hosts connect through switches, too many broadcast requests will slow down the network and in some cases, cause it to fail.

An easy fix for this problem is to break the network into smaller sections and then interconnect them using routers. Doing this disallows the transmission of broadcast packets across different networks, which thus breaks up broadcast domain collisions.

Apart from eliminating broadcast collisions in a network, a router also performs various operations such as:

- **Packet Filtering:** You can configure routers to drop packets based on certain criteria such as origin and destination. When you do this, the router acts as a firewall.

- **Path Selection:** If you are working with a network that has more than one router, they often communicate with each other to learn more about the connected networks and determine the best path to a certain host in the network.

- **Packet Switching:** Routers also work as switches by switching packets across the network. Doing this allows communication between hosts in the same network.

Now that you know how networks work and the various types of networks there are, we can move on and discuss the OSI model.

Section 2: OSI Model

#: The Open Systems Interconnections Model

The OSI model is a critical building block in the understanding of networking. In this chapter, we shall discuss the OSI model and specifically look at how it helps devices in the same network communicate.

We will start by discussing the reasons for using the OSI model. Then, we shall focus on the layers of the OSI models and explain how traffic flows between hosts in a network concerning the OSI model.

The primary factor behind the creation of the OSI model is to enhance communication across devices from various vendors. The OSI model also helps promote communication between hosts using different operating systems such as Windows, Linux, and OSX. Worth noting is that you will rarely encounter systems that natively utilize protocols that conform to the OSI reference model.

That notwithstanding, you need to understand the OSI model since other networking models such as the conventional TCP/IP build on the OSI reference model.

Like other networking models such as the Internet model, the OSI model operates by dividing the functions, the network protocols, and the devices in the network into various layers. Each of the Layers in the network model is responsible for certain network functions, and only the devices capable of performing this function reside in that layer.

Benefits Of Dividing A Network Into Various Layers

Dividing the network into various layers has various benefits such as:

- It makes troubleshooting easy: Communication in a layered network model further divides into small and simple components, which thus makes developing, deploying, and troubleshooting the network very easy.

- Because the network is layered, the vendors of various applications and devices only focus on writing the output and input specifications for the targeted layer. For example, a developer writing a web application does not need to know the specifications of an RJ 45 connector at Layer 1 of the OSI model. In such a case, this developer would focus on the layer related to the web application.

- Each layer functions independently; thus, changes in one layer do not affect the other layers in the network model. For example, a new wireless network does not affect how old applications run. An old version of Internet Explorer does not fail to run because the user is running a modern network connection.

- It makes standardization of functions divided into small independent sections easier.

- Layered networks let several categories of hardware and software, both new and old, to interconnect with each other flawlessly.

The OSI reference model constitutes seven layers that further fall into two groups.

1: The upper layers: This includes Layers 7, 6, and 5. These usually define how applications interact with the host interface, with each other, and the user.

2: The lower four layers: This includes Layers 4, 3, 2, and 1, which define the transmission of data between hosts in a network.

The figure below shows the seven layers, with a summary of the functions of each layer.

Application Layer - 7	Provides a user interface
Presentation Layer - 6	- presents data - performs encryption and decryption
Session Layer - 5	- maintains distinction between data of various applications - Maintains dialog control between hosts
Transport Layer - 4	- provides end-t--end connections - Maintains reliable or unreliable delivery and flow control
Network Layer - 3	- Responsible for logical addressing - provides path determination using logical addressing
Data Link Layer - 2	- provides media access and physical addresses
Physical Layer - 1	- transports data between hosts - converts digital data to be transported in a physical medium

Figure: Seven Layers of OSI Reference Model

Let's discuss each layer of the OSI model in detail:

1: Layer 7: Application Layer

The application layer is the topmost layer of the OSI model. It provides an interface between software applications on a specific host and the network.

On its own, the application layer does not include the software application; instead, it provides the underlying service required by the software. The best example is a browser such as Chrome or Mozilla Firefox and how it works.

When connecting to a website using such a browser, it utilizes the HTTP protocol that resides under the application layer of the OSI model to send and receive the contents of a requested webpage.

The HTTP protocol is available for use by various applications such as Opera, Internet Explorer, etc. However, the application —browser in this case— is not in the application layer.

On the other side of the webserver, applications such as NGINX, APACHE, or Microsoft IIS uses the same HTTP protocol to send and receive the HTTP requests from the browsers.

NOTE: The software application is not part of the OSI model.

2: Layer 6: Presentation Layer

As the name proposes, the presentation layer, which is the second topmost layer in the OSI model, is responsible for data presentation to the Application Layer.

The Presentation layers perform operations such as data encoding and translation. It takes data from the application layer and translates it into various generic formats that are then transported across the network.

Once the presentation Layer receives the data, it reformats the data into formats recognized by the Application Layer.

A popular example of this data translation and encoding is the **EBCDIC** to **ASCII** translation technique. The OSI model provides standardized protocols used to define how the formatting of the data.

It is good to note that the Presentation Layer is also responsible for data compression, decompression, encryption and also decryption.

3: Layer 5: Session Layer

The session layer is responsible for separating sessions of an application from others. For instance, different applications in a host, or, in some cases, different instances of the same application in a host might request and send data to and from the network. If this happens, the Session Layer is responsible for keeping the data from each requested session separate. It performs this by setting up, managing and terminating sessions.

It also helps establish and control dialogue between hosts as well as coordinate communications between systems in a network

4: Layer 4: Transport Layer

Unlike the layers above it, the transport layer, which deals with the applications and the data within the host connected to a network, mainly focuses on the definite end-to-end data transfer across the network.

The transport layer is responsible for the establishment of a logical connection between two interconnected hosts. It also provides a reliable and unreliable data delivery medium. The transport layer also provides easy and clean data flow as well as error recovery in the network.

Examples of Layer 4 are the User Datagram Protocol and the Transmission Control Protocol. It is, however, good to note that transport layers are not developed and do not conform to the OSI reference model.

5: Layer 3: Network Layer

To explain clearly what the Network layer of the OSI model does, we shall use an analogy.

Consider a scenario of someone mailing a letter via the postal service. After writing the letter, the first step is to place it in the envelope. The second step is to make sure you write down the destination address as well as the origin address so that the letter can return to you if undelivered.

In networking, this address is what we call a logical address, which is unique in that network.

Just as a street cannot have two similar addresses, in a network, each connected host has its own logical address. Once you hand over the letter to the postal service, it is the work of the postal service to determine the best path the letter should take to reach the specified destination. The same case applies in a network. However, in a network, the router needs to determine the best path it should use to reach the specified logical address. We call this process path determination.

In the final process, the postal service mails the letter using the path determined. Similarly, data moves across the network from point to point, mainly by routers until it reaches the correct destination.

The Network Layer of the OSI model completes functions performed by the postal service such as logical addressing, path determination and data forwarding to the correct address.

Routed protocols, used for logical addressing, and data forwarding and routing protocols used for correct path determination, are the two main protocols used in Layer 3 of the OSI model.

It is good to note that devices such as routers reside at the Network Layer. They, however, do not concern themselves with the destination host; they concern themselves with the destination network only. Tasks for host delivery are under the purview of the next layer of the OSI model, the Data Link Layer.

6: Layer 2: Data Link Layer

The Network layer is responsible for the movement of data across networks through logical addresses. On the other hand, the Data Link layer is responsible for the movement of data in a local network via physical addresses.

Every host connected to a network has a logical and physical address. The physical address is significant on a local network and unusable beyond the boundaries of the network. The data link layer also handles the protocol definitions used to send and receive data across a network media.

Earlier, we talked about how only a single host in the same network could send data packets at a time to avoid the data packets from colliding in a single domain collision. The Data Link layer helps determine when the transfer media is ready for the host to send the data packets. It is also responsible for detecting collisions in a network as well as the errors in received data. Devices that reside under the Data Link Layer include switches.

7: Layer 1: Physical Layer

The Physical layer, as the name suggests, deals with the transmission of data across a physical medium. Its functions include activating, maintaining and deactivating the physical medium between the connected systems. A router and a laptop are an example.

Critical elements of physical mediums such as ethernet cables are defined here. These elements include the voltage, connectors, the pin-outs, etc. The physical layer converts the received data to and from bit to electrical current for transportation across devices in the network. Hubs are popular devices that reside under this layer

#: Data Encapsulation

In the previous section, we discussed all the application layers and their functionalities relating to the OSI reference model. These layers work together —each with its functions— with the adjacent layer at the remote end. As an example, the application layer of the source host will only interact with the application layer of the remote host (destination).

For the operation to occur without any data corruption, each layer appends a header to the data received from the previous layer. The appended header contains information related to the protocol used by that specific layer of the OSI model.

The process the OSI model layers use to append a header to the data is referred to as data encapsulation. The header and the data sent from one layer of the OSI model to the lower Layer is known as a **Protocol Data Unit (PDU).**

The illustration below demonstrates how data gets encapsulated as it travels from the top to the last layer.

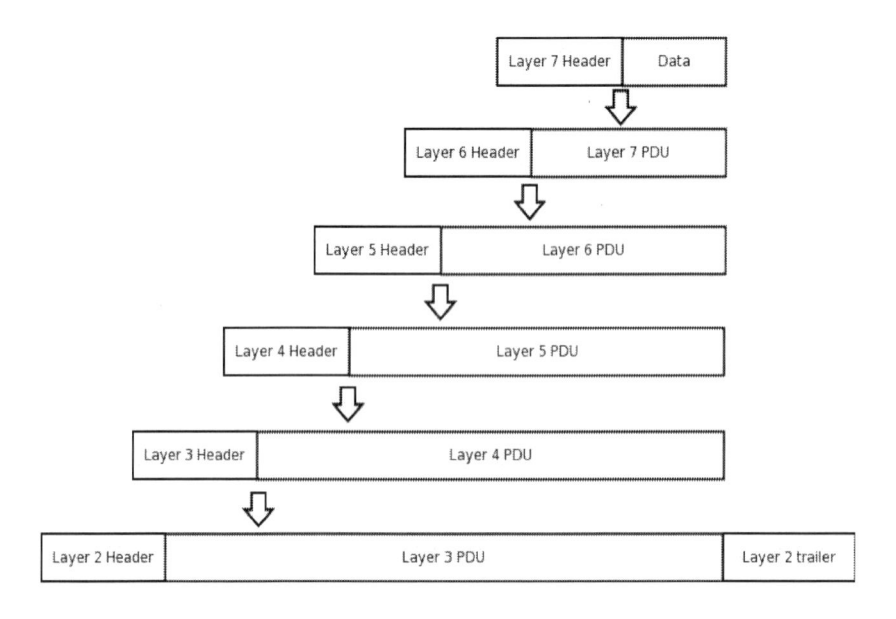

	Layer 7 Header	Data

⇩

Layer 6 Header	Layer 7 PDU

⇩

Layer 5 Header	Layer 6 PDU

⇩

Layer 4 Header	Layer 5 PDU

⇩

Layer 3 Header	Layer 4 PDU

⇩

Layer 2 Header	Layer 3 PDU	Layer 2 trailer

Encapsulation in the OSI Reference Model

At the source of the data, the Application layer appends a header containing the information about the protocol used creating a Layer 7 Protocol Data Unit. The Layer 7 PDU then passes down to the Presentation Layer. Layer 6 appends its header, which creates a Layer 6 PDU and passes it down to the Session Layer. This process repeats until the data reaches the last layer and passes through the medium to the destination.

After receiving the data, Layer 1 starts by taking off the data from the wire and pushes it up to layer 2. At Layer 2, the header is inspected and then removed —Layer 2 only reads Layer 2 PDU and removes it without changing the other headers. The remaining Layer 3 PDU then passes on to layer 3 where it is examined and removed. Layer 4, 5, 6, and finally 7 perform the same operation until the original data remains and is sent for processing by the appropriate application. The process of removing headers from the received data what we call data decapsulation

Section 3: TCP/IP

#: TCP/IP

As we discussed in previous sections, the OSI model and the TCP/IP model are the primary open standard networking reference models.

The two are similar, but one of them builds on the other. TCP/IP has, however, found more acceptance in modern networking concepts and thus, the TCP/IP protocol is the most used.

Similar to the OSI reference model, TCP/IP is a layered network model. In this section, we are going to cover the layers of the TCP/IP and how they work.

The TCP/IP model has 4 layers, which is different from the OSI model that has 7. The TCP/IP model is a more compressed version of the OSI model. The Layers in TCP/IP include:

1. Application Layer

2. Transport Layer

3. Internet Layer

4. Network Access Layer

Since the Four layers of the TCP/IP model are a compressed version of the OSI model, their functions are comparable to the Layers of the OSI model as shown in the figure below.

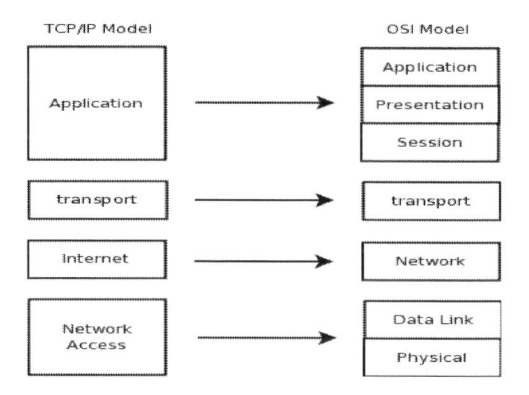

TCP/IP Model		OSI Model
Application	⟶	Application
		Presentation
		Session
transport	⟶	transport
Internet	⟶	Network
Network Access	⟶	Data Link
		Physical

Comparison between TCP/IP and OSI models

We will detailedly discuss the layers of the TCP/IP model and the protocols applied in each model.

1: Application Layer

The Application Layer of the TCP/IP model has the protocols used in the 3 top layers of the OSI model: the Application Layer, Presentation Layer, and Session Layers.

It performs functions such as interaction with the application, translating the data, data encoding, communication coordination, and dialogue control between the connected hosts.

There is a wide range of protocols used in the Application Layer of the TCP/IP model. The most common ones include:

HTTP

HTTP or HyperText Transfer Protocol is the most common protocol used in modern networks. HTTP is the building block of the World Wide Web (WWW) where its primary use is to transfer webpages from web servers also known as HTTP servers to the requesting client also known as an HTTP client.

Browsers such as Chrome, Firefox, Internet Explorer, etc, act as the HTTP client that allows you to connect to sites such as Facebook.com or any other site that is running on a web server such as Apache, NGINX, Tomcat, or Microsoft Internet Information Services. Although we have not covered ports, HTTP runs on port 80

Telnet

Telnet is a command-line protocol used to access the resources of remote hosts via the terminal. It involves the use of a client and a server. One host that acts as a Telnet server runs a telnet server daemon (application in Windows-based systems) and receives connections from remote hosts known as clients.

The Operating systems of the server present telnet connections via a terminal connection that uses only a keyboard and mouse. Telnet connections via CLI (Command Line Interface) are text-based and usually provide access to a command-line connection to the remote host. It is important to note that the client used, i.e., the application itself, has the name telnet on most Operating systems, but you should not confuse this with the Telnet Protocol. Telnet runs on port 23.

FTP

FTP is another commonly used protocol today. FTP or File Transfer Protocol's main use is the transfer of files between connected hosts. Like telnet and HTTP, FTP requires a Client and a Server. A host running the FTP daemon acts as the FTP server while the Clients connect via an application.

In most cases, a client connecting to an FTP service will need to authenticate via a username and a password before gaining access to the file structure of the remote host. Once connected, the client performs operations such view files and directories, upload and download files and other file supported functions. Similar to telnet, FTP applications are called ftp in most Operating systems; this does not mean they are the same as the FTP protocol. FTP runs on port 21.

SMTP

SMTP stands for Simple Mail Transfer Protocol. Its primary use is to send electronic mails. For example, when registering your email address via a Gmail app, you are using the SMTP protocol. In this case, the Client or the Application acts as the SMTP client.

SMTP is also the layer in use by mail servers to send and receive emails. However, the receiving client does not use SMTP to receive the emails; it uses POP3 instead. Standard ports for SMTP are: 587, 25 and 465

TFTP

TFTP or Trivial File Transfer Protocol is a more minimalist version of the FTP protocol. The central use of this fast protocol is uploading and downloading files.

Unlike FTP, TFTP does not allow a user to perform directory-related operations such as deleting, creating new directories, renaming, and more. TFTP has a major security issue since it does not require authentication to connect to the remote host and thus, its use is not common. TFTP mainly runs on port 69.

DNS

DNS or Domain Name System is also one of the most used protocols in networking. All the hosts connected to a network have a Logical address mainly known as an IP address – discussed in later sections.

IP addresses are mainly a bunch of numbers that are unique across one network. When connecting to websites such as google.com, you are connecting to a host (google servers) that have unique IP addresses. However, you do not have to memorize the IP address of every website you visit. (Machines do not understand names such as google.com and thus, they have to be converted to their respective IP addresses, which is where DNS comes into play.

Once you open a browser and type google.com, cisco.com, or any other web address, you send a DNS Query to a DNS server (provided by your ISP by default) which automatically converts the Domain Name to the IP address.

Once the DNS server replies to the IP address, a HTTP session to the requested server occurs, which allows you to connect to the site. On some sites, you may get a different IP address because of issues such as Load balancing. DNS runs on port 53.

DHCP

Dynamic Host Configuration Protocol simply called DHCP, is another useful protocol of the TCP/IP model. As we have discussed, every connected system in a network must have an IP address that distinguishes it from other hosts in the same network, thus allowing host-to-host communication. This logical address can be assigned to a connected host manually or automatically by protocols such as DHCP.

DHCP allows hosts to be connected to a network and assigned the logical IP address automatically.

To understand the importance of DHCP, imagine having to configure over 3000 hosts each with its unique IP addresses. Apart from IP addresses, each host has to be configured with the DNS server to use, the default gateway, subnet masks, and other critical information.

To avoid a lot of work for the users, DHCP automatically configures all the required information once a host connects to a network.

Now that we have discussed the Application Layer of the TCP/IP model, we can continue to discuss the next layer.

NOTE: All the protocols we have discussed in the previous sections are just a few of the many other protocols in that

Layer. Each protocol adds a header to the data that is passed through it and adds them moves down to the Transport Layer for transportation across the network to its specified destination.

2: Transport Layer

The name of the TCP/IP model transport layer is similar to that of the OSI model. The Transport layer concentrates on end-to-end data encryption and setting up logical connections between the connected hosts.

As we saw while discussing the OSI model, the Transport layer has TCP and UDP protocols. TCP is:

*A **connection-oriented**, **reliable** protocol that uses **windowing**, the process of taking a small subset of a larger dataset, for processing and analysis, to control the flow and provides **ordered delivery** of the data in segments. UDP, on the other hand, simply transfers the data without additional features or removal.*

Although TCP and UDP are unlike in several behaviors, they operate by performing their functions of transferring data using port numbers.

Before we move on to looking at TCP and UDP in detail, let us cover more about port numbers.

Port Numbers

A device connected to a network sends and receives a lot of data from other hosts at an instance. For that case, the system will probably have no way of defining which data belongs to which running application.

A solution for this comes in the form of protocols such as TCP and UDP using port numbers. They add a port number in the header of the incoming and outgoing data. Port numbers range from 0 to 65535. However, only 0-1024 ports are reserved for privileged services/applications. These ports are referred to as well-known ports.

Each application runs on its unique port number and is said to be listening on a certain port number. TCP and UDP protocol on the destination host will send the traffic to the specified port number added to the header.

At the origin, each TCP and UDP sessions gets assigned a random port number that is above the well-known port number. This allows the incoming traffic from the destination host to be identified on which application they belong to. The grouping of IP addresses, TCP and UDP protocols and the Port numbers of the hosts create a socket. The illustration below shows hosts sending and receiving traffic via TCP.

Cisco Networking Essentials

NOTE: In the Figure below, hosts on the left and right send traffic to the host at the center, which is destined for port 80 but from different port numbers. Due to the socket that makes the connections different, the host in the middle is capable of handling data from both hosts simultaneously.

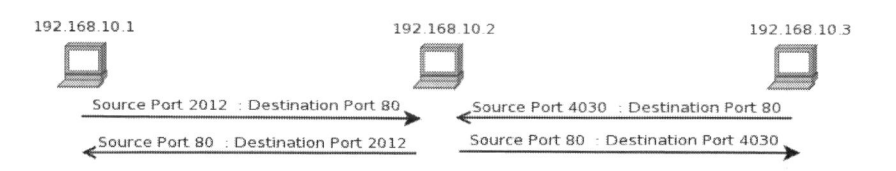

```
192.168.10.1              192.168.10.2              192.168.10.3

   Source Port 2012 : Destination Port 80    Source Port 4030 : Destination Port 80
   Source Port 80 : Destination Port 2012    Source Port 80 : Destination Port 4030
```

Multiple Sessions Using Port Numbers

The table below shows the transport layer protocol and port numbers used by different common application layer protocols.

Table 1-1 Well-known Port Numbers

Application Protocol	Transport Protocol	Port Number
HTTP	TCP	80
HTTPS	TCP	443
FTP (control)	TCP	21
FTP (data)	TCP	20
SSH	TCP	22
Telnet	TCP	23
DNS	TCP, UDP	53
SMTP	TCP	25
TFTP	UDP	69

NOTE: You must master the well-known port numbers and their respective services and applications.

Transport Control Protocol (TCP)

From the name, you can guess that the network Model (TCP/IP) TCP is one of the original protocols designed with the TCP/IP model, hence the name.

When sending data across the network, the application layer passes the data down to the transport layer for protocols such as UDP and TCP to transport it to the desired destination. TCP protocols start by establishing a virtual road or circuit between the source host and the destination host. We call this process a three-way handshake.

It then breaks down the data into small chunks called data segments and adds a header to each data chunk before finally passing in it down to the Internet Layer. The TCP header added to each data chunk (segment) is usually 20-25 bytes in size. The illustration below shows the format in which the headers are added.

NOTE: You do not have to remember the fields or the size of the TCP header formatting shown below.

Source Port (16 bits)	Destination Port (16 bits)
Sequence Number (32 bits)	
Acknowledgement Number (32 bits)	
Header (4 bits) / Reserved (6 bits) / Code Bits (6 bits)	Window (16bits)
Checksum (16bits)	Urgent (16bits)
Options (0 to 32 bits)	

TCP header process

Data is sent across the network by TCP protocol using the following sequence after being sent from the Application Layer.

Step 1: Connection Establishment

As discussed, the first step is to establish a virtual circuit between the source and destination hosts via the three-way handshake.

The three-way handshake operates using SYN and ACK flags in the Code Bits Section of the header (refer illustration above). This process helps set the sequence and acknowledgment number fields as the fields are vital to TCP.

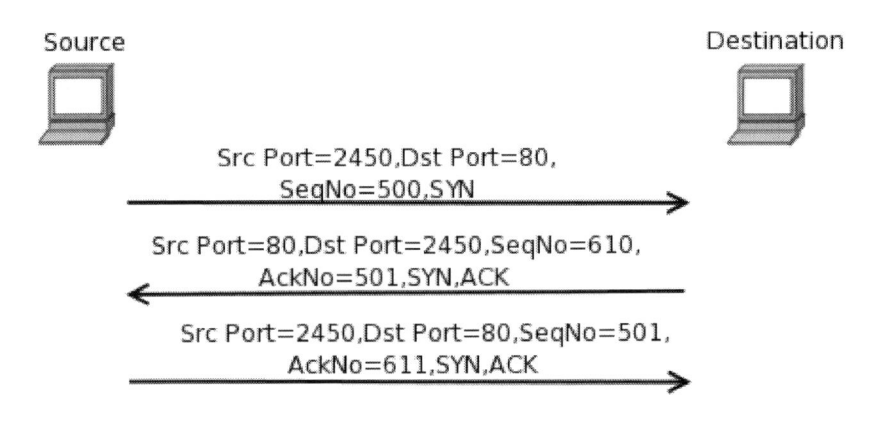

```
Source                                                    Destination

         Src Port=2450,Dst Port=80,
            SeqNo=500,SYN
         ──────────────────────────────►
         Src Port=80,Dst Port=2450,SeqNo=610,
            AckNo=501,SYN,ACK
         ◄──────────────────────────────
         Src Port=2450,Dst Port=80,SeqNo=501,
            AckNo=611,SYN,ACK
         ──────────────────────────────►
```

TCP three-way handshake

In the Illustration above, the source host starts by sending a TCP header to the destination host with a SYN (Synchronization) flag set. The SYNS request is a TCP packet sent from one device to another in the same network requesting that a connection be established between them. The destination host responds to the SYN flag with the SYN and the ACK (Acknowledgement) flags.

In the illustration above, the destination host uses the received sequence number + 1 as the ACK number because it is assumed that 1 byte of data was contained in the exchange of the headers.

Finally, the source host replies with only the ACK bit set, and the flow of data between the two hosts can start.

Step 2: Data Segmentation

The second function performed by the TCP protocol is data segmentation. The maximum size of data that is transferable across the network in a single Internet Layer PDU transaction depends on the protocol used in that layer. This maximum data limit is known as the Maximum Transmission Unit or MTU.

If the application layer sends to the transport layer data that is larger than the MTU limit, TCP breaks down the data into smaller segments limited by the MTU size. After breaking the data into segments, each byte of the data is identified using segment numbers. The arrangement of numbers in each header indicates the byte number of the first byte in that segment.

Step 3: Flow Control

The next step is flow control. The source host starts by sending data (segmented data) in groups. The header in the Window bit determines the total number of segments that can be sent at that specific time. This method helps avoid overloading the destination host which can lead to network failure. The window bit at the start is small but keeps growing as data keeps flowing.

Additionally, the destination host can request to slow down the data flow, thus avoiding overflow; the window is thus referred to as a sliding window. The source host cannot send further data segments until an acknowledgment response is received from the destination host if the host has sent the total number of segments allowed by the window.

The figure below shows the window increase during a data flow session. In the figure below, you will notice that the destination host increases the window from 10000 to 1200 when sending ACK back to the source host.

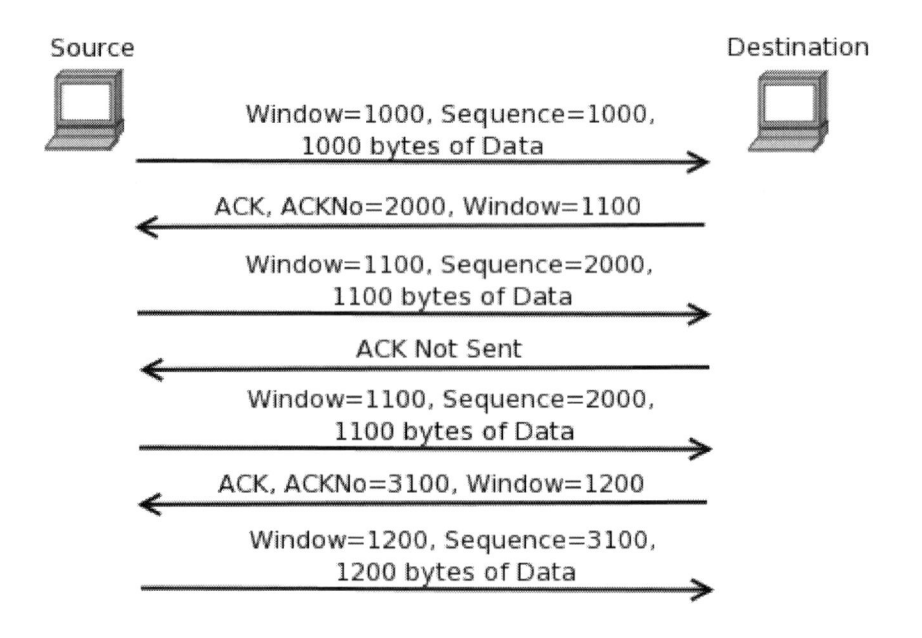

```
Source                                                    Destination

         Window=1000, Sequence=1000,
              1000 bytes of Data
         ──────────────────────────────────>

         ACK, ACKNo=2000, Window=1100
         <──────────────────────────────────

         Window=1100, Sequence=2000,
              1100 bytes of Data
         ──────────────────────────────────>

                  ACK Not Sent
         <──────────────────────────────────

         Window=1100, Sequence=2000,
              1100 bytes of Data
         ──────────────────────────────────>

         ACK, ACKNo=3100, Window=1200
         <──────────────────────────────────

         Window=1200, Sequence=3100,
              1200 bytes of Data
         ──────────────────────────────────>
```

TCP Sliding Window and Reliable delivery

Step 4: Reliable Delivery With Error Recovery

Upon data transfer completion, the destination host has to send an ACK flag to the source host indicating completion of data transfer. The ACK flag is set in the header and the ACK number is set as the sequence of the number of next bytes expected. The destination host does not send back the ACK flag if the correct number of segment bytes are not received. If the ACK flag is not received from the destination host, the source host knows that a number of segments were lost and thus retransmits the data segments.

Step 5: Ordered Delivery

TCP sends the data received from the Application layer in order and uses sequence numbers to mark the order in which the data has been received. Because of network issues, the data from the Application Layer can arrive in the wrong order. The work of the TCP protocol is to rearrange the data in the correct order and add the correct sequence numbers before sending the data. The order delivery and the sequence numbers are some of the benefits of TCP.

Step 6: Connection Termination

The last step in the transfer of data is connection termination. After the transfer of all the data, the TCP protocol initializes a four-way handshake to terminate the connection. To close a session, FIN (finish) and ACK request flags are used.

NOTE: TCP is one of the most essential protocols you need to learn before you can master networking.

User Datagram Protocol (UDP)

UDP is another protocol that is common in modern networking. TCP and UDP are very different in numerous ways. The only common aspect between TCP and UDP is their functionality of using port numbers to control the flow of data.

Unlike TCP that establishes connections and provides a reliable delivery path, UDP is connectionless and unreliable. It delivers data without overheads that are commonly associated with TCP protocol. Headers that are added by UDP contain only the source port of the data, the destination port, checksum, and the length. The length of a header added by UDP is 8 bytes in size.

Considering everything we have learned, it is easy to consider TCP as a better option to UDP. Since TCP is reliable and has more information in its header, which allows it to be more accurate, at first, it might seem like the better option.

However, it is essential to remember that modern networks are more stable than they were during the initial development of the TCP/IP model. TCP protocol has a larger overhead and the header contains more information and acknowledgments.

Since TCP protocol on the source host also holds data flow until an ACK flag is received, it mainly results in a delay that may be severe if a lot of information is flowing through the network. For example, in applications dealing with video and voice, UDP is preferable to TCP as it provides the application with the ability to be responsible for data reliability and thus fast data transport.

3: Internet Layer

This is next layer of the TCP/IP model. It receives all the data from the Transport Layer once TCP and UDP protocol has segmented the data and added the respective headers. If the destination resides in a different network from the original host and thus subdivided by routers, it is the work of the Internet Layer to ensure that the data segments are routed through different networks until the intended destination is reached.

The functions of the Internet layer in the TCP/IP model are similar to those of the Network Layer in the OSI model. The

Internet Layer provides function such as Logical addressing, forwarding, and path determination.

The most common protocols in the Internet Layer are Internet Protocol such as IP, Internet Control Message Protocol, or ICMP, which is used to send error messages across the Internet Layer and other routing protocols that help routers learn about the various networks they can reach.

Let us cover IP very briefly.

Internet Protocol (IP)

The Internet Layer of the TCP/IP model is controlled by Internet Protocol and other protocols that help in its functionality.

As discussed earlier, each device or host that connects to a network using the connected network interfaces of routers contains a unique logical address known as an IP address.

Hosts in a network are clustered in a single IP address range that is similar to a street address with every host having a unique marker from others in the same range. It is good to note that every network has various address ranges —devices such as routers operate in Layer 3 and help connect these different networks.

Once the Internet Protocol receives data segments from UDP and TCP, the IP appends its header that has the source Internet Protocol Address and the destination Internet Protocol Address along other information to create a PDU called a packet. Once the packet is forwarded to devices such as routers, the device checks for the destination address in the header and forwards it to the required network.

For that matter, a data packet can travel through multiple routers before arriving at the intended destination. Each router that a data packet goes through before arriving at its destination is known as a hop.

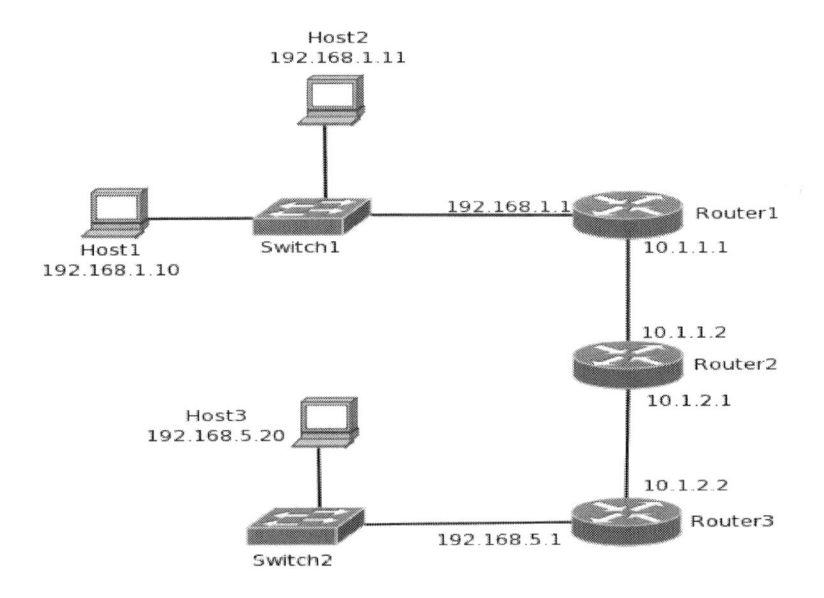

Packet flow in internetwork

To understand better how data is routed from one network to another, consider the above illustration. When Host1 sends data to Host2, it does not get routed as both Host1 and Host2 are in the same network range. Thus, the Data Link layer performs this action automatically.

However, if Host1 sends data to Host3, Host1 discovers that the destination host is in another network and will have to forward the data packet to Router1. Once Router1 receives the data, Router1 reads the packet header and determines the data packet needs forwarding to Router2.

Similarly, Router2 forwards the data to Router3, which is in the same network as the destination host, Host3. Once the data has reached Router3, the Data Link takes over and completes the delivery of the data to the required host. This entire process relies on IP address fields in the IP header of the data packet. Thus, IP addresses are important.

There are two main versions of internet Protocols: Internet Protocol Version 4, which is still in use but is gradually being replaced by the other version of Internet Protocol, Internet Protocol Version 6.

Cisco Networking Essentials

The figure below shows the header structure for IPv4

Bit 0	4	8	16	19	31
version	Header Length	Differentiated Services (DS) Field	total Length		
Identification			Flags	Fragment Offset	
Time to Live		Protocol	Header Checksum		
Source IP Address					
Destination IP Address					

Internet Protocol version4 Header

The fields that make up the IPv4 header include:

Version

The version field contains the Internet Protocol Version number. For IPv4, the value is 4; for IPv6, the value is 6.

Header Length

The header length field specifies the total size of the header itself. The minimum header size is 20 bytes. In the figure above, the rarely used option fields, a variable length, is not indicated. Most IPv4 headers are 20 bytes in size.

DS Field

DS or Differentiated Services Field is used to mark data packets. Various Quality-Of-Service (QoS) levels are applied to different markings. For example, a data packet going to video and audio protocols have relatively zero tolerance for delay.

The DS fields are used to indicate which packets are carrying data belonging to protocols that have zero delay tolerance so that they can get higher priority through the entire network flow. Traffic such as peer-to-peer is thought of as a major problem and thus marked down to give best-effort treatment.

Total Length

The total length field specifies the total size of the data packet, which includes the data and added headers.

Identification

Once the Internet Protocol has received the data from protocols such as TCP or UDP, it may require to break down the data segments into smaller chunks known as fragments before sending them through the network. The functionality of the Identification field is to identify the data fragments that make up the original data. Fragments of the same segment will contain the same identification number and thus joined together.

Flags

Flags are essential during the fragmentation process.

Fragment Offset

The Fragment Offset is used to recognize the fragment numbers. The destination hosts use it to reassemble the fragments in their right order.

Time to Live

TTL or Time to Live is a value set by the origination device to prevent packets from being transported across the network infinitely. Before the packet leaves the originating host, it is assigned a value for TTL. TTL value reduces by 1 for every router it passes. If the value reaches 0 before the packet reaches the destination, it is dropped.

Protocol

The protocol field helps identify which protocol the data belongs to. For example, a value such as 6 indicates the data has a TCP segment but a value like 17 is an indication of a UDP segment.

Besiddes UDP and TCP, data can belong to many other protocols.

Header Checksum

The header checksum helps with error checking. A cyclic Redundancy Check or CRC is performed on the data header at each router the data goes through as well as the destination host. The value return from the CRC check should be similar to the one stored in the Header checksum field. If the value is corrupted and therefore different from the value in the field, the data packet is discarded.

Source IP Address

The source field stores the source IP address of the packet.

Destination IP Address

The Destination field stores the destination IP address of the data packet.

The illustration below shows the usage of Source and Destination IP addresses in the transfer of the IP packet. Notice the destination and source addresses change during the data exchange between the two hosts.

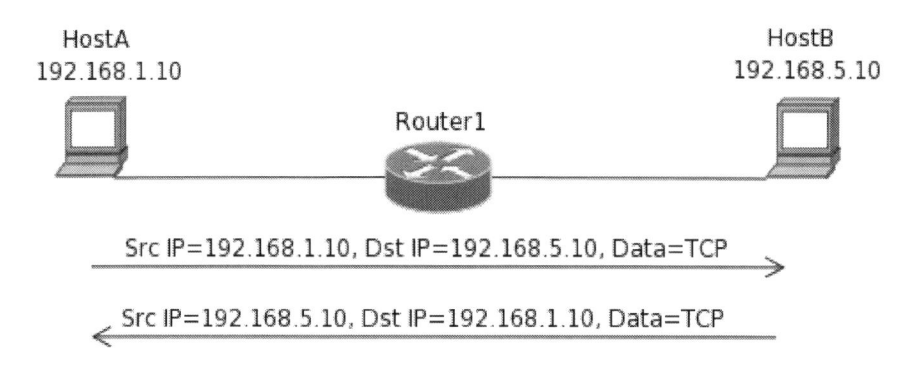

```
HostA                                              HostB
192.168.1.10                                       192.168.5.10
                        Router1

        Src IP=192.168.1.10, Dst IP=192.168.5.10, Data=TCP →
      ← Src IP=192.168.5.10, Dst IP=192.168.1.10, Data=TCP
```

Source and Destination IP address

Routing Protocols

In a previous section, we saw an illustration where Router1 needed to send data packets to Host3 via Router2. Router2, in turn, recognized that the packet had to pass through Router3.

To come to such logical decisions, routers utilize routing protocols stored in their routing tables. Routing tables contain all the information about the networks known to it — all the corresponding routers in the internetwork. Routing tables also have information such as the next router towards the destination networks.

As noted, these tables are created dynamically by routing protocols. We have numerous routing protocols that ensure routers are aware of the best path to all the networks.

Internet Control Message Protocol (ICMP)

ICMP protocol is a management protocol that acts as a messaging service for Internet Protocol. If the Internet Protocol comes across an error, it automatically sends an ICMP data in the form of an IP packet. There are various reasons why ICMP messages are generated. They include:

Destination Network Unreachable: If the data packet is unrouteable to the network where the destination IP address is located, the router drops the data packet and creates an ICMP message to the source host reporting the destination network is unreachable.

Time Exceeded: If the TTL of a data packet dies —reaches zero before the packet reaches its destination— and the router drops it, an ICMP message is generated and sent back to the source host to report that the TTL of the packet has expired and the packet has not been delivered.

Echo Reply: Performing Ping requests. ICMP messages are used to perform network connectivity checks. Utilities such as Pings use echo request to destination networks and hosts. Once the target receives the request, it replies by sending an echo reply to the source. If the echo request gets a reply, it indicates that the network is alive (available) and reacheable by the source network.

4: Network Access Layer

The Network Access Layer is the last Layer from the top of the TCP/IP model. It links the Physical and Data Link Layer of the OSU model.

This layer is responsible for protocols and hardware definitions required to connect a host to the physical network to deliver data. It receives data from the Internet Layer that deliver it through the physical network to the destination. The destination host can be a host in the network, or a router that forwards the data further. The Network Access Layer has a limitation to the physical layer defined by layer 3 devices such as routers.

This layer has a number of protocols. In a case such as a Local Area Network, Ethernet and its numerous variations are the most common protocol applied. Networks such as Wide Area Networks, Point-to-Point Network Protocols (PPP), and Frame Relay Protocols are in common use.

NOTE: In the next section, we are going to dive deep into Ethernet, its variations, and Cabling in general.

Before we dive deep into ethernet and Cabling, it is good to remember that:

1. Network Access Layer utilizes physical addresses such as Media Access Control Addresses (MAC) to identify the connected hosts and data delivery.

2. The header and the trailer of the Network Access Layer are only applicable in the physical layer. For that case, once the router receives the frame, it removes the existing header and trailer and appends the new header and trailer before forwarding it to the destination physical network.

3. A PDU from the Network Access Layer is referred to as a frame. A frame contains an IP Packet (from the Internet Layer), a protocol header, and a trailer from the NAC layer.

Section 4: Ethernet Technologies And Cabling

In this section, we are going to cover Ethernet and LAN cabling.

Before we get started, ensure you have understood the concepts discussed in previous sections because this section may refer to them several times.

Ethernet is a general term referring to a family of standards used to define the Network Access Layer for common types of Local Area Networks available in modern networking.

We have various ethernet standards that differ in terms of the supported network speeds, length and/or type of cables. The IEEE (The Institute of Electrical and Electronic Engineers), defines these standards.

NOTE: You can learn more about the IEEE from the following Wikipedia Page

http://bit.ly/2PycOy4

To understand the inner workings of the Ethernet, we will be referring to the OSI model instead of TCP/IP. TCP/IP combines both the Data Link and Physical Layer of the OSI model to form the Network Access Layer, which makes it more challenging to understand the functions of the Ethernet Fully.

Because we want to discuss the inner workings of the Ethernet, we shall use the OSI model for all our discussions in this section of the guide.

IEEE subdivides the functions of the Data Link Layer into two.

1. The 802.3 - Media Access Control (MAC) layer

2. The 802.2 - Logical Link Control (LLC) layer

Even though numerous physical layer ethernet standards are different with each requiring change at that layer, each uses the 802.3 header and the 802.2 LLC sublayer.

In the subsection that follows, we shall focus on collision detection mechanisms utilized by Ethernet and the functioning of Ethernet at each individually Layers.

Collision Detection In Ethernet

Ethernet is contention device. Contention is a type of media access method used to share broadcasting mediums.

The Contention media access method allows all the hosts in a specific network to share the total available bandwidth. This means that more than one host can use the same media for traffic transmission. However, if several hosts send traffic at the same instance, a network collision will occur, which will lead to the loss of the frames that collided.

Ethernet cannot prevent such scenarios. However, it is capable of detecting and taking corrective measures to resolve the issue. To perform this operation, ethernets use a protocol called a Carrier-Sense Multiple Access with Collision Detection or CSMA/CD. It is worth noting that despite the CSMA/DA protocol, it is only possible to minimize collisions, not completely remove them. Here is how the CSMA/CD protocol works:

Procedure For Initiating A Transmission:

1. Start by preparing the frame for transmission.

2. Listen if the Medium is busy (Ethernet)

3. If not busy, send the frame.

4. Source host Listens for collisions.

5. If a collision happens, the source host sends a jamming signal notifying all hosts of the happened collision. The jam signal is a signal that carries a 32bit binary pattern telling all other hosts in the network to stop transmission.

6. Source hosts in the network randomize a wait timer before resending the collided frame

Although the CSMA/CD works very efficiently at reducing collisions, it has several performance problems mainly because of:

1. Hosts wishing to send frames must wait until the transmission medium (Ethernet) is idle. This means that only a single host can send and/or receive frames at an instance –collision domain– such as networks connected to hubs. We call this logic a half-duplex. The image illustrates a Half-duplex.

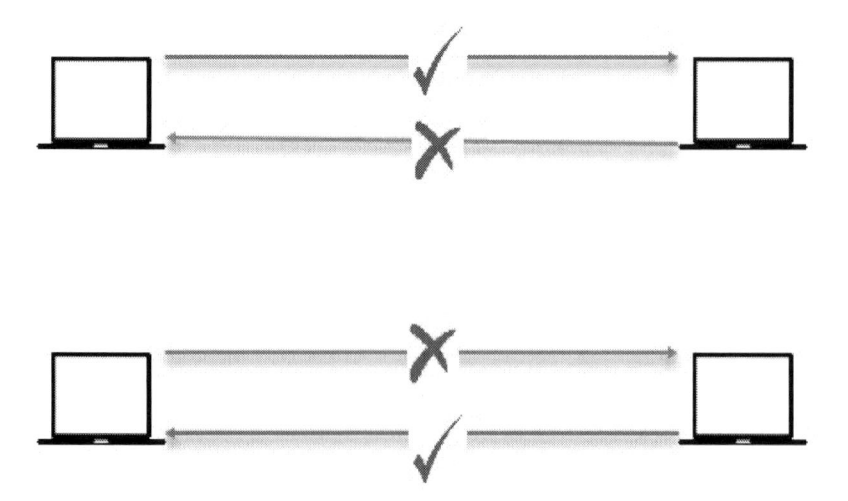

2. In case of a collision, no frames can be transported across the network. Even the host from which the collision frame

occurred has to wait for a random time before retransmission it is possible to retransmit the frame.

Worth noting is that until the introduction of switches, many networks experienced performance deprivation because of the usage of hubs.

Half And Full Duplex Ethernet

In a Half-Duplex, only one host is allowed to send or receive data frames at a single instance. Hosts are connected in half-duplex mode when in a hub-based network as they must detect collisions.

In a case where hosts connect via a switch, they can be set at full-duplex mode. Full-duplex mode means that the hosts can send as well as receive frames at the same instance without causing collisions.

Full-duplex uses two pairs of wire instead of one, thus creating a point-to-point connection between the transmitter (source host) and the receiver (destination host) and inversely. This means that the hosts send and receive data frames via different pairs of wire, which thus eliminates the need to listen to whether to send the frame or not. However, when Full-duplex is used, the CSMA/CD protocol is disabled on both ends.

Another advantage of the full-duplex method is that the devices can use twice the bandwidth available as each wire has the same bandwidth, and each wire is being used separately to receive and send data frames.

In the illustration below, the transmitter of the host's interface card is connected to the end receiver of the switch's interface and the receiver of the host's interface card is connected to the transmitter of the switch interface. This means that the traffic sent to and from the host both have dedicated paths with equal bandwidths. For example, if each path contains a bandwidth of 500 Mbps, the total dedicated bandwidth received by the host is at least 1 Gbps. If half-duplex was applied, only 500 Mbps would have been received for both sending and receiving the traffic.

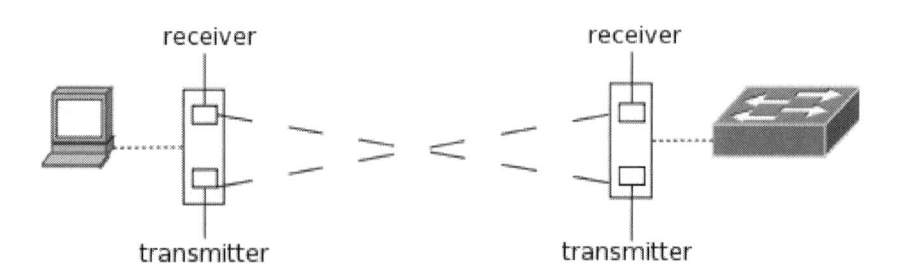

Ethernet At The Data Link Layer

At the Data Link Layer, the Ethernet is in control of addressing and framing the received packets from the

Network Layer. It also prepares the packets for the actual transmission.

Ethernet Addressing

Ethernet addresses that help identify a single or a group of devices on a Local Area Network are known as MAC addresses. A Media Access Control address is unique and is 48 bits long. It is written in hexadecimal format. Various devices and systems can write it in various formats.

For example, Cisco devices write it in a group of four hexadecimal digits separated by a period. Other systems such as common Operating Systems express it in groups of two digits separated by colons or dashes

Typical Cisco Mac Address: 00e0.04fe.63b9

Typical Windows Mac Address: 9B:D7:0E:96:44:8D or 9B-D7-0E-96-44-8D

An address used to identify a single device on the network is known as a unicast address. A unicast address identifies the source and destination of a data frame. Each Local Area Network card has a global unique MAC address. The IEEE conducts the Format and assignment of MAC addresses.

To keep the MAC addresses unique across the world, every manufacturer of Network Interface Cards gets assigned a unique code known as an OUI or Organization Unique Identifier. The OUI is then used as half of the MAC address while the other half is allocated by the manufacturer while ensuring that no similar half is used on more than one card. The unique MAC address is then encoded into the Firmware of the card.

The figure below shows the assigning of MAC addresses.

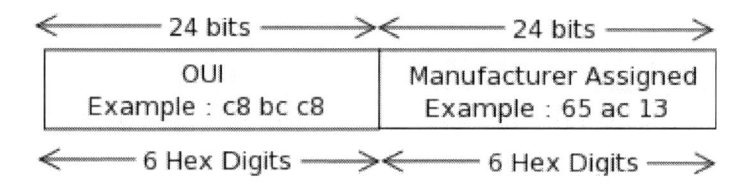

OUI	Manufacturer Assigned
Example : c8 bc c8	Example : 65 ac 13

←──── 24 bits ────→←──── 24 bits ────→
←──── 6 Hex Digits ────→←──── 6 Hex Digits ────→

48bit MAC address

MAC address also helps identify groups of devices on a network known as group addresses. We have two main types of group addresses defined by the IEEE. They include:

1. **Broadcast Addresses:** Broadcast addresses usually have a value of FF:FF:FF:FF:FF:FF, which indicates that all devices in that network should process the broadcasted frame.

2. **Multicast Addresses:** Multicast addresses are essential and in use when the sent frame needs processing by only a group of devices in that network. For example, when an IP multicast packet is to be sent via ethernet a multicast

of 00:E0:14:xx:xx:xx is used. XX:XX:XX, in this case, means that it can be any value.

Ethernet Framing

Once the data Link Layer receives a data packet from the Network Layer for transmission across the network, the Data Link Layer must encapsulate the packet into frames. These frames help identify the destination and the source devices by layer 2 devices such as switches. The frames also help the receiving host interpret the bits received by Layer 1.

Ethernet framing has changed substantially over the years. Xerox designed the original frame; however, it started changing more when the IEEE took over in the early 1980s and defined a new ethernet frame.

The figure below shows a finalized ethernet frame – includes the frame fields, size and description.

| Preamble 7 | SFD 1 | Destination Address - 6 | Source Address - 6 | Length/ type - 2 | Data 46 - 1500 | FCS 4 |

IEEE Frame

Field Name	Length (bytes)	Description
Preamble	7	Preamble field is used for bit-level data transmission synchronization and helps to the receiving device to identify where the header begins. It is also known as Syncword.
SFD	1	SFD or Start Frame Delimiter is used to mark the end of the preamble and indicates the beginning of an ethernet frame.
Destination Address	6	Used to identify the targeted destination address of the frame

Source Address	6	Used to identify the source address of the frame
Length	2	Used to indicate the length of the data field of the data frame. Contains either the length or type but not both
Type	2	Used to identify the Layer 3 protocol that is contained in the frame. Can be type or length but not both
Data	46-1500	Contains Layer 3 data
FCS	4	Used to store the CRC Checksum value which is used in checking for errors during transmission

Let us discuss the Length and Type fields a bit further.

Frame Fields

The type field is essential because it helps the receiving host identify the protocol whose data is in the frame. If the field value is less than 0600 hex or decimal 1536, it indicates that the field used a length field in the specific frame. If the field used is a length field, one or two headers are added after ethernet 802.3 header and before the layer 3 header. Thus, during the transmission of Internet Protocol packets, the ethernet frame contains two additional headers.

1. IEEE 802.2 Logical Link Control Header (LLCH).

2. IEEE Subnetwork Access Control Header (SNAPH)

The figure below shows an Ethernet Frame with LLC and SNAP headers.

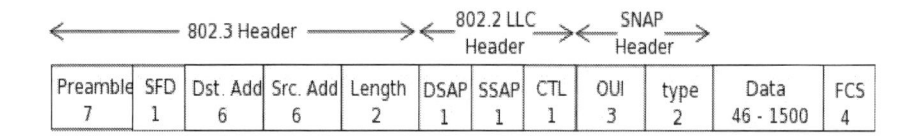

Preamble	SFD	Dst. Add	Src. Add	Length	DSAP	SSAP	CTL	OUI	type	Data	FCS
7	1	6	6	2	1	1	1	3	2	46 - 1500	4

← 802.3 Header → ← 802.2 LLC Header → ← SNAP Header →

802.3 Frame with LLC and SNAP header

Ethernet At The Physical Layer

A group of engineers from Digital, Intel, and Xerox is responsible for the initial development of ethernet. They created a 10Mbps ethernet using coaxial cables. The 802.3 ethernet standard come into being after the IEEE took over.

NOTE: Ethernet is a general term used to describe a family of standards such as Gigabit Ethernet, Fast Ethernet, Standard ethernet etc. We also use it to define the 10 Mbps ethernet variant.

The IEEE committee later grew to form new committees such as 802.3u, 802.3ab, and 802.3ae representing Fast Ethernet, Gigabit Ethernet, and 10Gbps Fiber and Coaxial respectively.

However, the Electronics Industries Association and the Newer Telecommunication Industries Alliance (EIA/TIA) are responsible for the creation of the physical layer specifications for the Ethernet. It requires a registered jack or RJ connector with a 45-wiring sequence on an unshielded twisted-pair (UTP) to be used on Ethernet. An RJ 45 cable is in a classified category. The higher categories have less of the following associated problems.

1. Crosstalk: This refers to undesirable signal interference from the adjacent pairs of the cable.

2. Attenuation: This refers to the loss of flux intensity (signal strength) while traveling through a medium (cables). We measure attenuation in decibels.

A cable in category 4 has lesser crosstalk and attenuation than a cable in category 2.

Now that we have discussed the bodies involved in the ethernet standards, let us look at the actual ethernet standards.

Section 5: Ethernet Standards

The table below shows the original ethernet standards. Each standard differs from the other in terms of Length, Speed, and Cable.

Name	Speed	Cable Type	Max Cable length	Connector	Description
10Base2	10Mbps	Coaxial	185 meters	AUI	Referred to as thinnet or Cheapernet. Supports up to 30 hosts in a single segment.
10Base5	10Mbps	Coaxial	500 meters	AUI	Referred to as *thicken*. Supports up to 100 hosts in a single segment.

| 10BaseT | 10Mbps | UTP | 100 meters | RJ45 | The first ethernet standard to use UTP cable. Requires the use of hubs for multiple hosts Host can be connected to a single segment or wire. |

original ethernet standards

The table below shows the Extended Ethernet Standards

Name	Speed	Cable Type	Maximum Cable Length	Connector
100BaseTX (IEEE 802.3u)	100 Mbps	UTP cat. 5, 6 or 7 two-pair wiring	100 meters	RJ45
100BaseFX (IEEE 802.3u)	100Mbps	Multimode Fiber	412 meters	ST or SC connector
1000BaseCX (IEEE 802.3z)	1000Mpbs	Copper twisted pair called twinax	25 meters	DE-9 or 8P8C

1000BaseSX (IEEE 802.3z)	1000Mbps	Multimode Fiber	220 meters	ST or SC connector
1000BaseLX (IEEE 802.3z)	1000Mpbs	Single mode Fiber	5km	ST or SC connector
1000BaseT (IEEE 802.3ab)	1000Mpbs	Cat 5 UTP	100 meters	RJ45

Extended Ethernet Standards

Ethernet Cabling

When connecting diverse kinds of devices with others, cabling techniques are necessary. We have three primary types of Ethernet cabling. They are:

1. Straight-through ethernet cabling

2. Crossover cabling

3. Rolled cabling

Let us discuss the three cabling methods below.

1: Straight-Though

A standard UTP cable has 8 wires. In straight-through cabling, we use 4 of these 8 wires. The arrangement of the wires on both ends of a straight-through cable appears in the figure below.

In the arrangement below, only wires 1, 2, 3 and 6 are in use, each connecting with the corresponding wire on each end.

```
1 ————————————— 1
2 ————————————— 2
3 ————————————— 3
6 ————————————— 6
```

Wire arrangement in Straight-Through cable

NOTE: The wire configuration is very important because the transmitter on one end connects to the receiver on the other end. In a case where the wires are arranged incorrectly, bits transmitted from one side will not be received on the other side.

2: Crossover

In crossover cabling, we use the similar four wires used in standard cabling. However, the connection of the pins is in a crossover. 1 is connected to 3, 2 to 6. The figure below illustrates a crossover cabling technique.

Cisco Networking Essentials

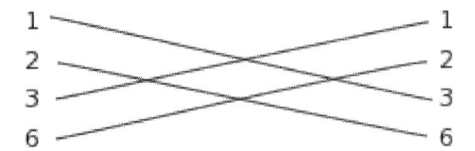

Crossover cabling wire arrangement

Crossover cabling works best when connecting:

1. A switch with another switch

2. A hub with a hub

3. Switch and a hub

4. Host and a Host

5. Router to Host

3: Rolled Cable

The Rolled cable technique usually comes into play when connecting to routers or switches' console ports from the host's COM port (serial communication port). Rolled cabling does not apply to ethernet connections.

Most Cisco routers or switches come with a console port used for the initial setup. In a rolled cable, we use all the wires, with each wire connecting to its opposite on the other end. 1 connects to 8, 2 connects to 7, 3 to 6, 4 to 5, etc.

The illustration below shows the arrangement of wires in a rolled cable.

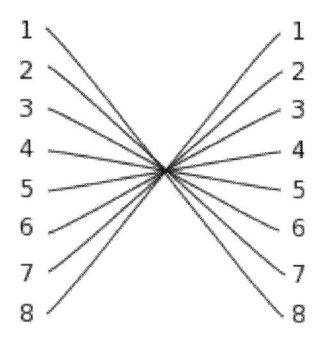

```
1           1
2           2
3           3
4           4
5           5
6           6
7           7
8           8
```

Rolled cable wire arrangement

NOTE: Types of cables and their specific area of usage is crucial in network engineering.

Section 6: Data Encapsulation In TCP/IP Model

The last concept to master about TCP/IP model is data encapsulation and PDUs. Data encapsulation in the TCP/IP is almost the same as in the OSI model. Data is encapsulated in a header and a trailer – for the Network Layer, creating a protocol Data Unit passed to the next layer.

Because we discussed the process in the OSI reference model, we will not discuss it again. However, you must know the names of the PDUs at each layer.

In the Transport Layer, the PDU is called A segment. Internet Layer the PDU is referred to as a Packet, and Finally, a PDU in the Network Layer is known as a frame.

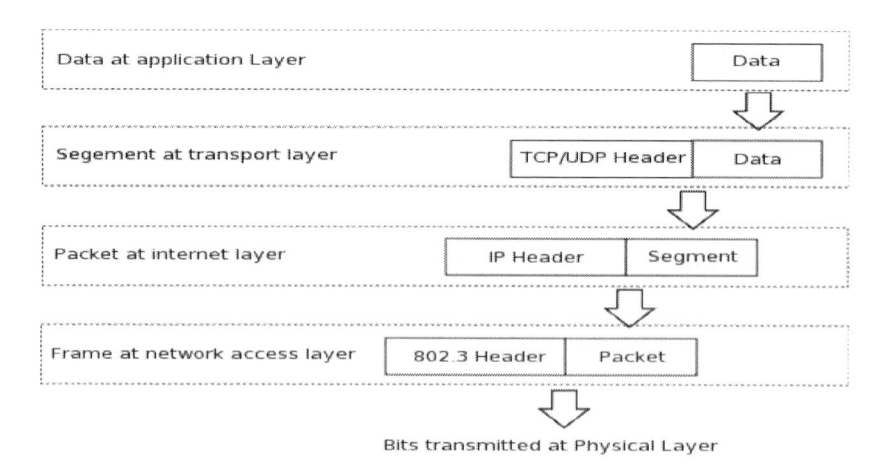

Data at application Layer		Data	
Segement at transport layer	TCP/UDP Header	Data	
Packet at internet layer	IP Header	Segment	
Frame at network access layer	802.3 Header	Packet	

Bits transmitted at Physical Layer

Data encapsulation in TCP/IP Model

Cisco 3 Layer Hierarchical Model

Large establishments have large and complicated networking models comprised of numerous numbers of protocols, services, devices, and locations. Upgrading complex networks is very often challenging.

However, thanks to Cisco's expertise in network equipment and network management, they developed a 3-Layer hierarchical model. Such a model creates a modular and hierarchical methodology of networking building that makes it easier to manage, scale, upgrade, and troubleshoot networks.

Cisco Layer 3 Model breaks internetworks into three main Layer:

1. Core Layer
2. Distribution Layer
3. Access Layer

However, these layers are only logical with specific functions in an internetwork. Let us discuss the features of each layer.

1: The Core Layer

The core layer of the three-layer model acts as the backbone of the internetwork. It is a simple but very critical layer that performs functions such as transporting large amounts of data at fast speeds. It works by getting data from the distribution layer and sending it back after transportation. This layer offers fast speeds and robust fault tolerances since it transports large amounts of data and any network faults affect every connected host. Because of the critical functions of this layer, you should avoid the following:

1. Avoid direct user connections to this layer

2. Avoid Direct Server connections

3. Avoid Complex service policies

4. Avoid slow traffic actions such as inter-VLAN routing, packet-filtering, etc.

Before developing a core layer, you should consider the following factors:

- Ensure to include redundancy in this layer

- NAL technologies must be fast and low latency

- Low coverage time for routing protocols.

2: The Distribution Layer

The distribution layer acts as an intermediary between the core Layer and the Access Layer. Its functions include providing routing, WAN access, filtering, as well as determining how packets access the core layer if required. It also provides other essential functions such as path determination, which provides the fastest way access requested is completed. It also performs as a merging point for access layer switches. The following are some of the functions performed at this layer.

- Breaking broadcast in the domains.

- Routing subnets and VLANs

- Route distribution between routing protocols.

- Execution of security policies such as address translations, firewalls, packet filtering, etc

3: The Access Layer

This Layer contains the edge of the network where devices such as Personal Computers, Mobile devices, printers, etc resides. Resources required by users is accessible in the layer. Access request to remote resources is forwarded to the distribution layer. Access Layer is also known as the desktop layer. The Access Layer has the following functions:

- Dynamic Host Configuration Mechanisms

- Static routing and ethernet switching

- Access control

- Controlling collision domains.

Here is a short recap of basic terms you need to master to internalize Ethernet technoligies.

- Network Address: in routing, a network address is a remote network. For example, hosts in remote networks are within network addresses.

- Bit: A bit refers to a single digit whose value is 1 or 0

- Byte: A byte is a unit of data made up of 8 bits.

- Broadcast Address: A broadcast address refers to the address used to send data to all connected hosts in the network. The default broadcast address is 255.255.255.255.

- Octet: This is a unit of data comprised of 8 bits. While discussing IP addresses, we use byte and octet interchangeably.

In the next section, we shall discuss Internet Protocol Addresses.

Section 7: Internet Protocol Addresses

#: IP Addresses

Previous sections have discussed IPs on a surface level.

An IP address is a 32-bit long digit. For easier reading of the IP addresses, it is divided into four sections, each section being 8 bit long. Each 8-bit long section of an IP address is divided by a period. This makes each section 1 octet/byte long. IP addresses are natively expressed as binary numbers. However, to make them easy to remember, they are converted to decimal values.

For example, an IP address such 11000000101010000000000001001001 is divided into 4 sections making 11000000.10101000.00000000.01001001. If this IP address is converted into a decimal, it ends up being 192.168.0.73. The decimal format of an IP address is referred to as a dotted animal. Other applications also convert an IP address in hexadecimal and Octal format.

This chapter relates significantly to the conversion of binary to decimal IP addresses and vice versa. The table below shows decimal values in each bit location in a byte. This helps in the conversion of IP addresses.

To convert a binary IP address into its decimal format, simply add up the decimal value that corresponds to the bit place in (1). For example, a binary of 10110000 is 128 + 32 +16 = 176 in decimal.

| 128 | 64 | 32 | 16 | 8 | 4 | 2 | 1 |

Decimal Value for each bit place in a byte

In common networking scenarios, you will encounter various, common binary decimals as shown in the table below.

Binary Value	Decimal Value
10000000	128
11000000	192
11100000	224
11110000	240
11111000	248
11111100	252
11111110	254
11111111	255

Decimal Values for common binary numbers

IP addresses do represent more than the host addresses; they also contain information about which network the host resides. This is usually in two main parts of the IP address.

1. The Network: Used to represent the network (subnet of the network) in which the host exists in.

2. Host: This component represents the host in the network

The combination of both the network component and the host component is unique in the entire network. To identify the section that relates to the network and the one that relates to the host component of the IP address, the IP address is classified in the five main classes discussed below

Class A

In a Class A address, the first 8 bits represent the network component, while the remaining 24 bits represent the host component. In binary, this is equal to a range of 1 to 127 addresses. However, we have exceptions such as 127.x.x.x.x and 0.x.x.x.x which are reserved for the loopback and the default network.

Therefore, a Class A address is in the form of 126.255.255.255.255 where 126 is the network component and the rest 255 values denote the host component.

Class B

In Class B addresses, the first 16 bits represent the network portion while the remaining bytes represent the host section.

Class C

In Class C addresses, the first 24 bits represent the network section while the last 8 bits represent the host section.

Class D

Class D addresses are ideal for multicast and other known protocols such as OSPF or Link-Local Multicasts.

Class E

Reserved addresses for addresses such as broadcasts.

Hence in a binary IP address first 5 bits of the IP address and the first octet in a decimal IP address represent the Class of the Address. The table below shows the range of classes.

Class	First 5 bits in binary	First Octet range
A	0xxxx	0-127 (actually 1-126 because 0 and 127 are reserved)
B	10xxx	128-191
C	110xx	192-223
D	1110x	224-239
E	1111x	240-254

Address range for different classes of address

NOTE: You must remember the Classes of addresses and their respective address ranges. Before moving ahead, spend some time figuring out the class of some addresses given below. Also, try to figure out which portion is the network and which piece is the host part:

Some IP addresses, such as 127.0.0.1, have a special meaning.

Cisco Networking Essentials

The table below lists such addresses and what they represent.

Address	Representation	Usage
The network starts with all Zeros	Characterizes "any network." 0.0.0.120 is a goo example	Used to transport broadcast messages to the entire network.
The network starts with all Ones	Indicates all networks	Used to send a broadcasted message to all networks.
Nodes containing all Zeros	Indicates a network address or all hosts in the network	Used by a router to route traffic across networks
Nodes containing all Ones	Represents all hosts in a network —also referred to as the broadcast address	Used to send broadcasted messages to all hosts in the network.
Entire address of	Represents "any	Label default

83

os	network."	route
Entire IP set to all 1s.	Indicates all hosts in the network.	Used to deliver broadcast requests.
127.0.0.1	Represent the loopback address – represent the host itself	Used to send traffic to and from the localhost. For example, when running a local server, you will use this address in the host browser.

Reserved IP addresses

Conclusion

Thank you for reading this guide.

We trust that it has been helpful and that it has helped you learn everything you needed to know about cisco networking. As is the case with most things, to master what you have learned in this book, you need to read and then test your understanding of the material.

I'd like your feedback. If you are happy with this book, please leave a review on Amazon.

Please leave a review for this book on Amazon by visiting the page below:

https://amzn.to/2VMR5qr

Printed in Great Britain
by Amazon